A *mostly* KIDS' GUIDE TO
SANIBEL & CAPTIVA ISLANDS
AND THE FORT MYERS COAST

Karen T. Bartlett
Adventurer in Chief

Karen T. Bartlett

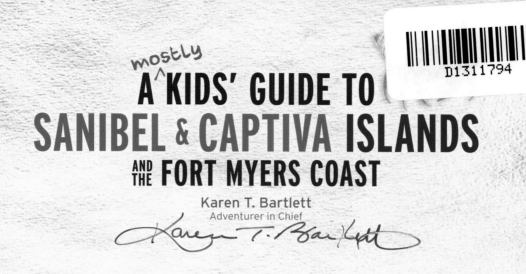

Inspired by the never-ending story of
adventure and discovery with the loves of my life,
Christopher Y. Bartlett and Sarah Rose Bartlett

Mostly Kids Guides LLC

First published October 2016 by
Mostly Kids Guides LLC
6141 Pelican Bay Blvd, #19; Naples, FL 34108

10 9 8 7 6 5 4 3 2 1

Cover Illustrations: Margie Olsen and Terri Rickman
Design and Production: Christine Rooney and Brad Sanders
Maps: Margie Olsen, Randall Simmons and Christine Rooney
Photography: Karen T. Bartlett except where otherwise credited
Content Advisors: Christopher Y. Bartlett and Sarah R. Bartlett
Research and Editorial Assistant: Kira Pirre

To purchase additional copies of this book, to schedule an event, or for information about special volume discounts, contact Karen T. Bartlett
(239) 595-9026
mostlykidsguides@gmail.com

 @kidsguides Mostly Kids Guides

ISBN 978-0-9909731-5-7

Who will love this book?

- ✓ Grandmothers
- ✓ Teachers
- ☐ Manatees
- ✓ Little Kids
- ✓ Medium Size Kids
- ✓ Big Kids
- ✓ Moms & Dads
- ☐ Raccoons
- ✓ Librarians
- ☐ The Man in the Moon
- ✓ Tour Guides
- ✓ Concierges
- ☐ Dolphins
- ✓ Realtors
- ✓ Grandfathers
- ✓ Aunts & Uncles

"I love this book!"

CONTENTS

Stuff you Need to Know

Some of it is quite weird.

2,000-pound mermaid? Well, yes and no. In 1493, Christopher Columbus wrote in his ship's log: *"...the Admiral said he quite distinctly saw three mermaids...but they are not so beautiful as they are said to be."*

Look, fingernails! Just like mermaids!

Frank Brinker

What did he really see? Manatees! They eat about **150 pounds** of sea grass a day so they're also called **sea cows.** Actually, they're related to elephants.

Manatees are gentle and curious about people. They hang out in shallow water around docks, and in creeks and bays. **They swim v–e–r–y slowly,** *(you would too if you weighed a ton),* so it's hard for them to get out of the way of their worst enemy: boat propellers.

Whoa! Did he just see a manatee?

MANATEE ZONE
30 MPH IN CHANNEL
SLOW SPEED OUT
OF CHANNEL

Certificate of Adoption

The bearer of this document is an Official Adoptive Parent of

ROSIE

an endangered West Indian manatee

at Homosassa Springs Wildlife State Park

Jimmy Buffett, Co-Chairman,
SMC Board of Directors

Save the Manatee Club • www.savethemanatee.org

Rosie was the Mostly Kids Tribe's very first **adopted manatee** from the Save the Manatee Club. This year we adopted Ariel. We think they are as **beautiful as mermaids.**

*"You can recognize roseate spoonbills by the excellent **spoon at the end of our beaks**. It's very helpful to scoop up delicious **shrimp soup** in shallow water. We live all over the islands."*

Spoonbill

Not a Spoonbill

This is a flamingo. Any flamingos you see around here are either very lost or **very plastic.**

Ever see these **long, snaky vines** growing out of the dunes like they're trying to escape down the beach for a swim? A **railroad vine** can grow so fast you can almost *(but not quite)* see it grow!

giant bundles of grass

Seminole chickee roof

Q: When is a tree NOT a tree?
A: When it's a Palm Tree!

The **state tree of Florida** is a palm tree. **But here's the thing:** Palm trees aren't trees. They're nothing but **giant bundles of grass!** Seminole Indians used the fronds of Florida's state *not-tree* to build their traditional homes, called **chickees.**

Doggy Love

Dogs on leashes are welcome on all county beaches. But for serious swimming, running and ball-chasing awesomeness, head straight to **Dog Beach** near **Lovers Key**. It's free!

Sagittarius

Wow! Look up in the sky!

Meteors, planets and shooting stars shine brightest over dark beaches and wilderness spaces. See them at **the Calusa Planetarium**, or meet up with **real astronomers with giant telescopes** for a night adventure.

Bald eagles are **giant raptors** descended from **dinosaurs,** and they still have **superpowers.** Like diving for fish at 100 miles per hour! They build ginormous nests - some as big as the inside of a car. People all over the world watch Fort Myers' famous bald eagles, Harriet and M15, on the **Southwest Florida Eagle Cam.** We even get to **watch their eggs hatch** and see the baby eaglets learn to fly.

M15

Harriet

E8   E7

True or False? Biologists don't approve of naming wild animals. Most creatures that are rescued or tracked get numbers only. **Answer ⬇**

True! But Harriet is extra special.

Ospreys are raptors too, but not as huge. Look for their stick-like nests in dead tree branches and on channel markers. Both ospreys and bald eagles eat mostly fish, but bald eagles also love snakes, frogs, small animals and **vulture vomit.**

↗ gross

Please don't eat these oats.

They're **way** too scratchy! Besides, sea oats help save sand dunes from erosion, so it's against the law to pick them. **Legends say that if you hang a shell on a tree at the beach, you're sure to return some day.** Sea oats are way too fragile, though, so find a nice sturdy mangrove to hang your shell!

Don't eat sea grapes either!

(Unless they're in a jar of jelly, yum!) But the leaves are very important! Some say that pirates used their daggers to scrape secret messages into the leaves. **Try it!**

"But not with a dagger, please! Use a sharp shell!"

The letters will turn white at first, and then disappear in a few days.

Tourist Tree?

Its real name is gumbo limbo, but the nickname "tourist tree" comes from its **red, peeling skin**, like a sunburn. Pretty funny, huh?

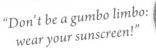

"Don't be a gumbo limbo: wear your sunscreen!"

Butterflies!

Sometimes they flutter by. Once in a while they sit on your nose. We have gazillions of butterflies because we have gazillions of delicious flowers, in the wild and in special **butterfly gardens.**

7

You can be a Junior Ranger!

Sign up **free** at any state or national park (including preserves and refuges) for cool ranger programs, activities & fun stuff!

EVERY KID IN A PARK

FREE PASS ALERT!

All **4th graders** get a free pass into **national parks** for the whole year!

Pete Sottong

recycle fishing line here

Going Fishing?

Kids under 16, Florida grownups over 65, and people fishing with licensed guides **don't need a fishing license.** All Florida residents can fish from the beach for free. *Everybody else: get a license!*

*"Be an **environmentalist**! Please recycle any no-good fishing line you find on the beach so we don't get tangled up or choke on it."*

QUIZ

an environmentalist is
a. someone who reads minds
b. someone who loves nature & wildlife
c. a very long word

answer: b and c

Ancient Indians & Dastardly Pirates

Way before the Seminole Indians, the Spanish Conquistadors and the pirates who looted treasure ships, lived the ancient Calusa Indians, the fiercest warriors in the history of Florida. The Conquistadors told their queen that they were giants and cannibals.

Were they really cannibals? Who knows? But they Loved seafood! For thousands of years, they feasted on clams, oysters and whelks. They used the shells to carve fishhooks, spears and ceremonial masks. Sometimes the leftover shells made mounds so high that whole islands were formed.

Fun idea: Sign up for a guided Calusa tour with Gaea Guides, Captiva Cruises or Calusa Ghost Tours.

Jolly Roger, designed by Calico Jack

Not a real pirate, but she *IS* from England, just like Calico Jack!

Buried Treasure

Yes! Girl Pirates!

Fearsome pirates like Calico Jack Rackham and his pirate wife, Anne Bonny attacked many Spanish galleons filled with gold sailing past these islands. Some say there's still buried treasure at their old hideouts on every island in this book. Black Caesar once looted 14 tons of silver. His hideout is named Black Island. Could that be where he hid the booty? And what about all the treasure ships sunk in hurricanes? Their gold has never been found either... YET!

"Conquistador" means "conqueror," but Ponce de Leon made a HUGE MISTAKE when he tried to conquer the Calusas. He was killed by a Calusa arrow.

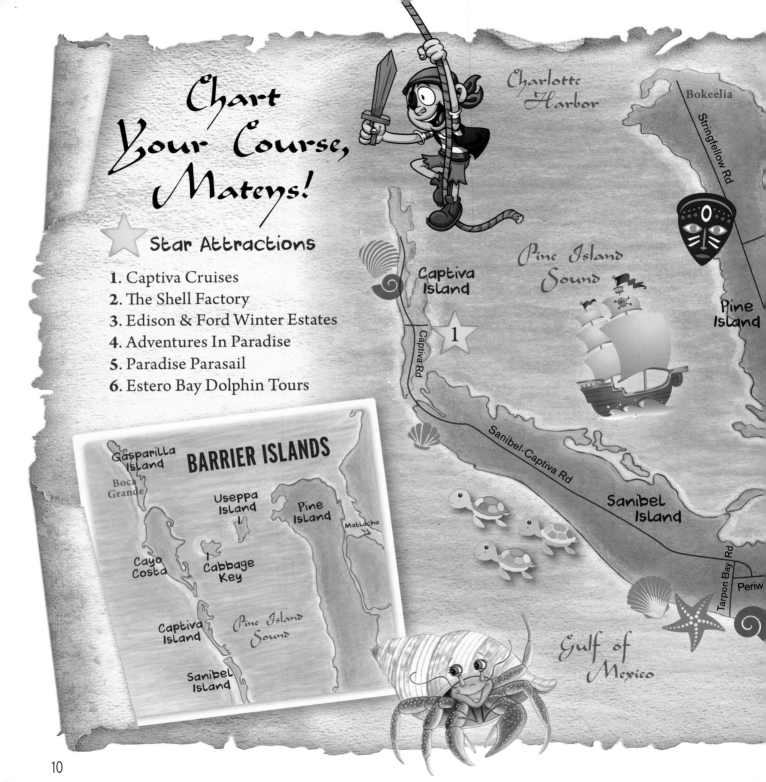

Chart Your Course, Mateys!

⭐ Star Attractions

1. Captiva Cruises
2. The Shell Factory
3. Edison & Ford Winter Estates
4. Adventures In Paradise
5. Paradise Parasail
6. Estero Bay Dolphin Tours

BARRIER ISLANDS

Gasparilla Island
Boca Grande
Cayo Costa
Useppa Island
Cabbage Key
Pine Island
Matlacha
Captiva Island
Pine Island Sound
Sanibel Island

Charlotte Harbor

Bokeelia

Stringfellow Rd

Captiva Island

Pine Island Sound

Pine Island

Captiva Rd

1

Sanibel-Captiva Rd

Sanibel Island

Tarpon Bay Rd

Periw

Gulf of Mexico

Pine Island Rd

Downtown
Fort Myers

75

Veterans Memorial Pkwy

Cape Coral

Caloosahatchee River

McGregor Blvd

Colonial Blvd

Gladiolus Dr

Alico Rd

Summerlin Rd

San Carlos Blvd

41

Fort Myers Beach

Estero Bay

Estero
Island

Estero Blvd

Lover's
Key

2

3

4

5

6

Sanibel Island

The Scoop, the Stoop and the Poop

Everybodys doing the Sanibel Stoop!

About **six bazillion seashells** wash up on Sanibel every year – more than any other island. Why? For one thing, Sanibel sits sideways, making it one **big, curvy scoop** net! The tide tosses shells up, but takes only some of them back. Some are rolling around in the water, some are covered in dry sand, and some are **live creatures hiding** in the wet sand from birds that would like to eat them for lunch. **How do you find them?**

Do the Sanibel Stoop! Just walk along the beach, **folded in half like a taco,** and look sharp! That's it – you're doing the Sanibel Stoop. It's even in the **Guinness Book of World Records!**

HEAD-TO-HEAD

AMERICAN CROCODILE
Crocodylus acutus

AMERICAN ALLIGATOR
Alligator mississippiensis

Q: Are there differences between **alligators** and **crocodiles**?

A: Yes, some very "sharp" ones (like teeth – get it?). Get the **inside scoop** about gators and crocs and a whole lot more at "Ding" Darling National Wildlife Refuge.

"Excuse me. Sanibel isn't totally about seashells. There are exciting adventures, beautiful birds (just saying), and things to see, including - if you can believe it - fancy **boxes of bird poop.** *It's quite embarrassing."*

poop

scoop
net

Who loves this kind of **scoop**?

Sanibel and Captiva have the most **dee-licious** homemade ice cream. Try a **Love Boat** scoop, a **Royal Scoop** scoop, a scoop of **Queenie's Famous Ice Cream**, or a scoop with a curl at good old **Dairy Queen**. At **Pinocchio's**, every scoop is topped with an animal cracker.

13

A Shelliferous Place!

Besides colorful (and sometimes totally unbelievable) shells and creature exhibits at **The Bailey-Matthews National Shell Museum,** you can watch some pretty awesome **mollusks** moving around in the live tank and learn **freaky factoids** to impress your teacher!

Check out the cool kids' craft days!

Live Mollusk Tank

Look and Discover what a live mollusk does under the water.

LIVE MOLLUSK OBSERVATION TANK

PLEASE:
• Don't touch the water.
• Do not remove animals from water.
• Do not splash water.
• Do not put anything into tank.

The Calusa Indians in this exhibit look so real that people actually talk to them. *Then they feel a little silly.*

biologists who study mollusks and conchs

Besides the scientific names that **malacologists and conchologists** use, everyday folks know shells by their everyday names. Like **baby's ears** and kitten's paws, **angel wings** and turkey wings, **horse conchs** and fighting conchs, jewel boxes, **tulips** and buttercups, olives and **figs!**

Okay, what's a mollusk (and what's not)?

Glad you asked! It's a **squishy creature** with a head and **one foot (but no legs).** The shell is its skeleton!
The foot is a piece of shell attached to the squishy part that they use to walk underwater and on the beach.
Some mollusks **(like an octopus)** have no shells, so they sometimes hang out in other mollusks' empty shells.

So, whose shell is this, really?

I'm a fighting conch

(a true mollusk). This is my **natural born shell.**
I'm **pretty gorgeous** if I do say so myself.

I'm a hermit crab

(not a mollusk) camping out in
a fighting conch shell. It's like having
my own **mobile home.** Check out
my **be-yoo-tiful** green eyes!

Guess what?
**If you find a junonia
shell (a true mollusk),
you get your picture
in the newspaper!**

Not a mollusk

Can you find the
**Live sea urchin
(not a mollusk)** hiding
under the shells?

Whoa!
Blue crab with **BIG pinchers!**
Best to scoop up in net, look and release.

Wrack, Wrack, Wrack

Smelly Alert! Wrack lines can get kind of stinky.

Live shelling: DON'T DO IT! That goes for sea stars, too! Live shelling is against the law.

Wrack is a line of sea life the tide leaves behind. Birds skitter around in it looking for **small crabs, dead fish** and other **tasty treats.** Look closely! You may find a sea star, or a baby seahorse or even a **purple blob** like this one discovered by the kids at **Sanibel Sea School** camp. It's called **sea pork.** Maybe it should be called **zombie brain.**

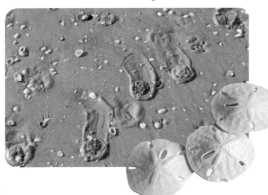

Sign up for a super-cool beach camp or a beachcombing adventure with **real biologists and naturalists** at several of the **nature centers and guides** in this book

"Don't forget my frie Pam, Sanibel's world famou shell guide, a iloveshelling.cc

Sand dollars can WALK?

Yes, seriously! They have thousands of fuzzy spines that work like legs. These guys got stranded on the beach and are walking back to the sea.

Olive Shell digging a tunnel back to the sea ↘

If they're **smooth** on the bottom, they're okay to take. Soak them in bleach water to make them white.

BEACHES! So many awesome beaches!

Lighthouse →

Once upon a time, Sanibel needed a Lighthouse...

...to guide ships safely into port. **But guess what?** The ship bringing all the parts sank! How's that for **bad luck?** Luckily, divers rescued the pieces.

Flocks of birds hang out at the **Lighthouse Beach pier**, waiting for fishermen to drop some **juicy bait!** Other **great fishing spots** are the bays, the Causeway islands and the Blind Pass bridge. Actually, practically anywhere there's water.

Beach Umbrella

Not an Umbrella — *it's a Reddish Egret*

Dolphin! ↓

Family alert!

Bowman's Beach is Sanibel's **largest beach park**, with a playground, picnic areas and more. *See all the beaches on page 76.*

Capt. Rob Modys

Redfish!

Dolphins & Puffer Fish & Seahorses, oh My!

Okay, adventurers! Grab your **mucky-muck shoes** and hop aboard the big yellow catamaran for an **Adventures in Paradise Sea Life Encounter.** Watch for **dolphins playing**, or even following your boat. You're headed for a **desert island,** so get ready for surprises! When you land on the island, grab your scoop net and follow the sandy path to the beach. Wade right into the shallow water and gently **swoosh your net** through the soft sea grass.

You might catch a **tiny shrimp** or **crab**, a **king's crown shell** with the creature still inside, or even a **seahorse!**

But the adventure's not over!

Who knows what kinds of fish or **outrageous new creatures** your guide may scoop up in the boat's net! **Like this pufferfish!**

Say hi to the creatures, take a picture, and then **back they go into their habitat.** What a day!

John Debidetto

"Attention Grownups!
Adventures in Paradise also has shelling, fishing and dolphin watching cruises, and island trolley tours."

19

Attention humans!

The **alligators, raccoons, skunks** and **Brazilian free-tailed bats** at **"Ding" Darling National Wildlife Refuge** have a message for you:

Friday is creatures' day off.

So on Fridays, don't even THINK about getting on the **Wildlife Drive.**
Any other day, come on in! Of course, humans are welcome any day in the **Visitor Education Center.**

IT'S FREE!

and the other
47,507
bazillion creatures
More or less.

Don't forget to pick up you[r]
free Junior Range[r]
at the welcome des[k]

Check out the colossal **manatee skeletons, alligator and crocodile skulls,** and lots more, plus super-fun **interactive habitats** and animal exhibits.

"Ding" Darling National Wildlife Refuge

The refuge has lots of inside and outside happenings, like boardwalks through the mangroves, bike paths, movies, and kids' crafts every week.

Our very favorite thing is the Scat Walk! (That's the biology word for poop). It's like a treasure hunt, without silver and gold. Each box along the boardwalk has a goopy looking splat or a poop pile like one made by a bird or animal. For real! Sometimes you can see pieces of **undigested bones** or feathers. Try to guess who did it, and then open the box to find out! Great stuff for a school report, right? Be sure to climb the observation tower at the end of the boardwalk for an awesome birds-eye view of the refuge.

eeeewww!

"DING" DARLING DAYS

LET'S GO OUTSIDE!

"Ding" Darling Days

Free Family Fun Day is "Ding" Darling's best day of the year. The **all-day festival** has **animal programs**, art, music, face painting, **hot dogs**, a butterfly house, **tram tours**, goodie bags and lots of surprise happenings. Blue Goose will be there to pose with you for selfies. It's all totally free.

Shhhh! Masked bandits may be watching!

It's **so peaceful** kayaking through the **mangrove forest.** No sound except the plop/splash of your paddle. You're all alone in the refuge, right? Wrong! **Who's that masked bandit** staring at you from the mangrove roots? Just a **raccoon,** hunting for a delicious seafood breakfast! Are those **dolphins jumping** over there, and is that a manatee swimming up to check you out? And wow, look at the **great egret** standing like a statue in the shallow water!

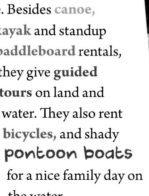

Q: Who has the head of a horse, the tail of a monkey, and the pouch of a kangaroo?

A: A seahorse! It's true. And guess what else! The father seahorse has the babies!

Tarpon Bay Explorers is the official outfitter of "Ding" Darling National Wildlife Refuge. Besides **canoe, kayak** and standup **paddleboard** rentals, they give **guided tours** on land and water. They also rent **bicycles,** and shady **pontoon boats** for a nice family day on the water.

Q: What creature always sleeps with one eye open?

A: "**Me!** *Come to the free Deck Talks at Tarpon Bay Explorers to find out more* **bizarre** *things about us dolphins and other creatures in the Refuge."*

23

CROW? That's the Center for the Rehabilitation Of Wildlife

If you were an **eagle with a broken wing**, a pelican with a **fishhook** in your stomach, or a **bobcat** that was hit by a car, you'd want to go straight to the CROW animal hospital. Just like people hospitals, CROW has **x-ray equipment, operating rooms** and special **hospital beds** for each kind of creature. Even bathtubs! Healed animals get released back into the wild.

Can you believe it?
More than **4,000 wild animals** come to CROW every year!

"Kids at least age 13 (with a grownup) can sign up for a special tour of the hospital and rehab areas."

Gopher Tortoise
(Gopherus polyphemus)

Attention future veterinarians! In CROW's visitor center, you can watch live patient cams, read the doctor's **charts**, play "Be the Vet" and "Surgical Challenge" **interactive games**, meet **animal ambassadors** and more. Kids 12 & Under are free!

24

300-Pound
Prehistoric Sea Turtles Invade the Islands!

Looks like monster truck tracks!

can weigh 300 pounds

I ounce

Ginormous loggerhead turtles are descended from prehistoric ancestors that lived **40 million years ago.** Mama loggerheads swim thousands of miles through the ocean each spring to **crawl onto the beach** and dig nests. They deposit about 100 eggs each. **Imagine: 600 nests a year adds up to 60,000 eggs!**

The baby turtles all hatch together. They **erupt like a volcano** from the nest and race for the sea as fast as their tiny flippers can go. Later, an expert turtle team counts the empty shells, and **rescues any hatchlings** that got stuck inside.

"Sea turtles can only crawl forward, and will get stuck on things in their way, so please fill in the moat around your sandcastle."

Kids love watching the rescues.
This lucky hatchling and lucky boy get a selfie together before the release.

SCCF for short

The turtle team at **Sanibel–Captiva Conservation Foundation** watches over the nests to help protect them from their **worst enemies:** raccoons, **fire ants** and **ghost crabs.** Sometimes even people. It's against the law to disturb sea turtle nests.

SCCF also keeps track of manatees, **snakes,** frogs and other creatures. Check out the **nature center** with its **butterfly garden** and **observation tower.** Kids under 17 get in free. They also have **boat** and **kayak tours** and **wading trips.**

What a view!

Did you know? Sea turtles love to swim. Gopher tortoises definitely do not!

So what ELSE is there to do?

"PLENTY! May I suggest..."

See an awesome show

See the exciting holiday show and family plays at BIG ARTS' Herb Strauss Theater. And don't miss the **children's theater productions,** starring kids and teens.

QUIZ

Who has the right of wa bicycles or creatures?

Correct: it's **always creature** Watch for gopher tortoises strolling along the bike path!

Take a family bike ride

Bicycles are definitely the most fun and easiest way to get around. Sanibel has **25 miles of bike paths,** and not a single traffic light. Go straight to **Finnimore's Cycle Shop** or **Billy's Rentals** for bikes for every size (helmets included, of course) including bicycles for two, beach wheelchairs and training wheels. Billy's even has **Segways** (age 14 and up). Finnimore's also has **paddleboards & boogie boards.**

Take breaks for souvenirs, supplies, lunch or a picnic at one of the **beach parks.** Sanibel Community Playground is shady and **little-kid friendly.**

Be a pirate

Go on Captain Bubby's Pirate Scavenger Hunt. On this exciting **private family adventure,** you get your own pirate name, a pirate treasure map, and **loot to take home.** Captain Bubby knows tons of **pirate secrets** and **bizarre nature stuff.** Like, **why snowy egrets wear yellow slippers!**

Sorry, we can't reveal the answer.

"Psst mateys, I'll tell ye! That feathered scallywag wiggles its spiky *yellow toes* in the water to *freak out the fish,* and then he snatches some up for lunch!"

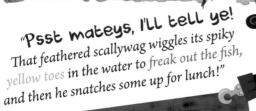

Check out the pioneer museum

Wonder what Sanibel was like in pioneer days? Visit the old **post office, gas station, schoolhouse** and more at the **Sanibel Historical Museum & Village.** Learn about the island's black pioneer families, and see some of the strange stuff that was for sale 100 years ago at the first Bailey's General Store.

They didn't sell fancy chocolates like Bailey's does today, **but look! Good old Hershey's Kisses!**

Anything Else? Well, how about a speedboat ride?

Q: What's the fastest way to circumnavigate Sanibel and Captiva Islands?

That means "sail all the way around."

A: Aboard the Sanibel Thriller. It kicks up tons of spray, but you won't even get wet. Everybody from **babies to teenagers to grandmas** love it!

Taste goodies at the Farmer's Market
Every Sunday except in summer.

Purple and Orange cauliflower? Seriously! And so good!

Yes! FREE Pizza samples!

Mmmmm... Cake Samples!

Slices $4

Chocolate Felony Cake

Visit the parrots at Jerry's Shopping Center
Some of them talk. This cutie pie is named Babe.

Meet some Monkey

Who knew? A campground where you can visit monkeys and parrots, and **it's free!** Check out **Periwinkle Park Campground** and **Wildlife Park**. You might even get to hold a bird.

Read a book

Wait. Those are donuts and shells.

What's the deal?

In summer, Bennett's Donut Shop gives a **free donut to kids** who read a book in their reading corner. Check out the **crazy flavors** like peanut butter S'mores or **maple bacon**.

The Sanibel Public Library has **books**, **storytimes** and other fun **activities**, and they also have an awesome seashell collection.

Go to the movies

You won't find a cute movie house like the Island Cinema in any big city! It's very comfy, but small, so arrive early to get a seat!

Be the last ones on the beach

Sunset is a great time for shelling. And guess what? The most **plendiferous colors** happen AFTER sunset. It's called afterglow.

"Orange and purple cauliflower? Bacon donut? Birds with yellow slippers?

If you think THOSE are crazy, turn the page!"

Bubble Scouts? Crab Races? Skeleton Fishermen?
What kind of a place IS this?

Captiva Island once was like the Wild West: Calusa Indians **battling** Conquistadors, pirates hiding captives, and **Seminole Indian raids.** Luckily, not all at the same time. And there were **shipwrecks.** In fact, the first settler floated ashore on a piece of wood! Nowadays, the wildest things are dolphins and seagulls.

← That's why it's named Captiva

↙ And Bubble Scouts!

It's true! At the **Bubble Room, the weirdest restaurant on the planet,** waiters wear decks of cards and chickens on their heads. Inside are **Superman's phone booth, Santa's workshop,** and you won't believe what else. Just trying to see it all makes us dizzy.

Captiva gets all magical in December with its Holiday Village, boat parade, fireworks, and goofy **golf cart parade.**

"Rudolphin? Now THAT's funny!"

WAITING FOR BIG SHRIMP
GoCaptiva.com

Two great selfie spots at Jensen Marina!

Laugh till your teeth fall out at the hilarious **crab races**, Wednesdays in season at Tween Waters.

Grownup Alert: be sure to choose the **family** show!

h, yes, you can atch **some big ones** in ine Island Sound, in the backwaters and e Gulf of Mexico!

Courtesy photo: Capt. Rob Modys

Chapel by the Sea is the pioneer church and cemetery. Next door, inside the library, is a teeny-tiny but **very clever museum**, built like the inside of the island's **old mail boat**.

31

Everything's more colorful on Captiva!

Do you love big boats or small ones?

Do you prefer watching the sunset, or watching the night sky for shooting stars? Would you rather go **shark fishing**, kayaking or wildlife-watching? On Captiva you have so many choices!

Find **fantastic fishing guides**, boat rides & rentals, and a tiny but cool fishing museum at **Jensen's Marina.** Charter a **private sailing or fishing trip**, or join a **kayak adventure** at **Tween Waters Marina.** First time kayaker? No problem – it's easy!

manatee

Lady Chadwick has morning, sunset and even night-time astronomy sails from South Seas Resort.

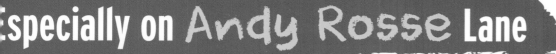

That's the main street of **Captiva Village**. It's just two blocks long, but it is loaded with fun things to do, tasty treats, cool shops, and a few bizarre things too. When you're exploring, see if you can find the **camel**, the **frog**, or the **yellow brick road!**

Island people love **wild and crazy mailboxes.**

Captiva has no mailboxes except this big one at the post office, but wait till you see the ones on Sanibel! This **purple mermaid** is our favorite! Can you find the **pink flamingo**, the **lighthouse**, the **guitar** or the **big red clock**?

"Hey kids, why not mail a postcard to me, Freckles, at the Captiva Post Office? My address is on page 2."

Don't forget to wave to your friends on the **Mucky Duck BeachCam.** If you stay for sunset, be sure to watch for the green flash!

Shore birds, especially gulls and terns, are used to people. If they get startled while trying to rest or fish, they fly up in a rush and then get too tired to fish. Island kids try to be respectful of their space and tiptoe by.

What's up with that green flash? Every once in a while, just at that place where the sun sets on the horizon, there's a bright green glow. Many people have never seen it. If you do, you're very lucky.

A super fun day at the beach

Sunrise to sunset awesomeness

At the end of Andy Rosse Lane, you'll step right into the sand. A few more hops, and you'll end up with your toes in the Gulf of Mexico! What's there to do? Why, swimming, **sandcastle building**, shelling and seagull watching, to start! Have you tried stand-up paddleboarding or parasailing? How about a **WaveRunner** or banana boat ride?

WOW! You can even wade out to the hot dog boat!

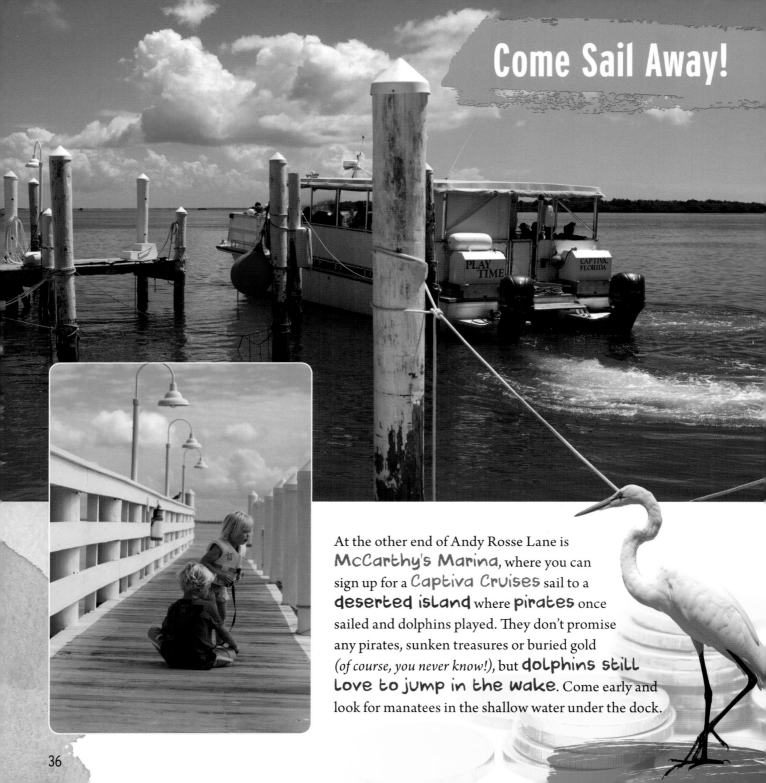

Come Sail Away!

At the other end of Andy Rosse Lane is McCarthy's Marina, where you can sign up for a Captiva Cruises sail to a deserted island where pirates once sailed and dolphins played. They don't promise any pirates, sunken treasures or buried gold (*of course, you never know!*), but dolphins still love to jump in the wake. Come early and look for manatees in the shallow water under the dock.

Meet the captain (and maybe help him drive the boat!)

Pack a picnic! Take a swim! Go beachcombing with a **real naturalist** who knows the names of all the shells.

Real naturalist!

PLAY TIME

iLoveShelling.com

QUIZ

a wake is

a. the opposite of "a sleep" (get it? asleep – awake!)
b. lake, spelled wrong
c. the waves a boat makes

answer: c

Mysteries of the Barrier Islands

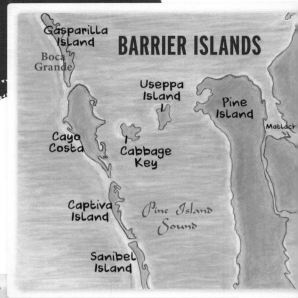

BARRIER ISLANDS

Who wants to camp at the beach, toast marshmallows around the campfire, and sleep under the stars? Who wants to stand on top of an ancient **Calusa shell mound?** Who wants to take a boat ride to see dolphins and seabirds, and **white pelicans** as tall as a third-grader? Who wants to search for sea stars, whelk eggs and **prehistoric horseshoe crabs?** Everybody, right?

So, just hop on a boat and go!

QUIZ

Horseshoe crabs aren't crabs! They're related to

a) horses
b) spiders
c) stingrays

Surprise! The answer is b

BRIDGE OR NO BRIDGE?

Pine Island and Gasparilla Island have bridges like Sanibel, Captiva and Fort Myers Beach. But Cayo Costa and Cabbage Key: by boat only!

Horseshoe crabs lay thousands of eggs that look like tiny squishy green grapes— kind of like spider eggs!

Horseshoe crab, dolphin - Shutterstock

How would you like to live in this fish house?

whelk

moon snail

sea star

Bring your snorkel!

Cayo Costa
So much to do!

Rent a bike and ride the sandy trails. Check out the pioneer cemetery. See if you spot a **wild hog!**
Dig in the sand. Play in the water. Go fishing. Camp out! Besides tent sites, Cayo Costa has primitive cabins to rent. And we mean **seriously primitive,** like **cold showers only!**

Whelk eggs inside!

Skeletons and Ghosts (well, sort of!)

WOW! Look what happens when islands get **smacked by big hurricanes.** These mangrove **tree skeletons,** all bleached in the sun, look kind of cool, don't you think? And guess what? You can find shells, **seaweed,** and even **tiny crabs** hiding in the roots!

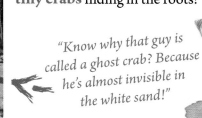

"Know why that guy is called a ghost crab? Because he's almost invisible in the white sand!"

Way-cool boat trip to
Cabbage Key

Woo Hoo!
Going camping on
Cayo Costa!

Cabbage Key is a **tiny island** with nature trails, an old fishing lodge and a restaurant. A long time ago, when a fisherman made lots of money selling his fish, he tacked a **dollar bill on the wall** with his name on it. Why? In case if one day he didn't catch any fish to sell, he could just use his dollar bill to pay for his lunch. Now, everybody does it! There are at least 27 trillion dollar bills on the walls and hanging from the ceiling.

Be sure to climb to the top of the **water tower.** And watch for white pelicans and dolphins on the boat trip!

Boat Alert!
Attention Grownups: Here are some of the boat operators for these barrier islands.

Captiva Cruises
Captiva to Boca Grande, Cayo Costa & Cabbage Key

Island Girl
Pine Island to Cabbage Key & Boca Grande

Captain Jack Boat Tours
Pine Island to Cabbage Key

Tropic Star
Pine Island to Cayo Costa & Cabbage Key

Whoa! Can you believe a 10-foot wingspan?

Shutterstock

Tell your parents:
People say that Jimmy Buffet wrote his famous song, **"Cheeseburger in Paradise"** when he tasted the delicious cheeseburgers at Cabbage Key! They make yummy Key lime pie, too!

It's true! Trick your friends with this question!

QUIZ
Key Lime juice is
a) kind of yellow
b) bright purple
c) lime green

Answer: a

Pine Island
and Wacky Matlacha

← Matla-cha rhymes with Satur-day

There are no more pirate hideouts on Pine Island (that we know of!) but wait till you see **Matlacha,** one of the wackiest villages in the **entire solar system.** You won't believe the weird back garden at the Lovegrove Gallery. Blue bottle bushes? Pink palm trees? You can paint a face on a coconut, write your address on the back of its head and mail it to yourself! Or maybe join **Captain Jack** for a ride in the **craziest painted boat** ever!

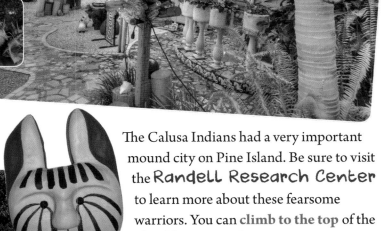

The Calusa Indians had a very important mound city on Pine Island. Be sure to visit the **Randell Research Center** to learn more about these fearsome warriors. You can **climb to the top** of the **shell mounds** that took more than a thousand years to pile up!

Eco-Awesome!

Manatees, dolphins, turtles and big fish hang out in the **Matlacha Pass Aquatic Preserve.** Watch for raccoons, great blue herons and other **creatures hiding in the roots** of the shady mangrove tunnels. Check out **Gulf Coast Kayak** for super-fun kayak and SUP tours.

ON TOP OF THE WORLD

Imagine yourself at the top of an ancient Calusa town.

YOU ARE HERE

PINE ISLAND SOUND

Ancient Recycling! First they ate the seafood, then they recycled the shells! How smart is that?

Gasparilla Island

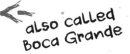 also called Boca Grande

How much do you weigh? **Can you imagine catching a 250-pound fish?** Giant tarpon live in deep **underwater holes** around Gasparilla Island. Each June, kids age 15 and under can sign up for the **world's biggest kids-only tarpon fishing tournament.**

Better start practicing now! Check out the special Family Day on the Water with **Florida Inshore Xtream Charters**, or super kid-friendly **Captain Chris** at **Reel Intense Inshore Charters**.

Get it? Fishing REEL!

Important rules!

You can look, but please don't touch; chase, feed, or give water to us.

Your help will safeguard manatees from harm.

Thanks for caring!

Stingray

Look for the wild iguanas!

Is the whole island about fishing? Noooo!

You can get bikes or a **golf cart** at rental places like **Island Bike 'N Beach** near the old train depot, and ride to the lighthouse at **Gasparilla Island State Park** for beachcombing, a **picnic** and a **swim**. The top of the lighthouse is open only one day each April during the Lighthouse Birthday Party. Before heading home, try a dee-licious scoop of **ice cream** at the **Pink Pony** or the **Loose Caboose**.

Fort Myers Beach
Outrage-alicious!

Grab your flip-flops, your coolest shades, and a big bucket of imagination—and get ready to discover the most outrage-alicious beach town in Florida!

Watch for pirate ships and shrimp boats. You might see a totem pole... or a giraffe... and who knows what else! Look at all the colorful rooftops! Check the sky for sea gulls, pelicans and colorful parasails.

Ready? Set? Put on your sunscreen and GO!

Shutterstock

43

First Stop: Times Square. The center of the universe on Fort Myers Beach is a **big blue clock** at Times Square. From there you can do just about everything: play at the beach, see what the fishermen are catching on **the pier,** get a **slice of pizza** or a strawberry smoothie.

But that's not all—especially at the Friday and Saturday **sunset celebrations.** You might see a three foot-tall **blue macaw** with **yellow eyes,** a **silly mime,** a street **musician,** or a **juggler** wheeling around on a **unicycle.**

Good Idea: keep some **coins in your pocket** to drop in their baskets.

Shutterstock

This way-cool information booth at Time Square is named **Roxie!**

and other fantastical things!

Have you met the Fort Myers Beach
Shrimp Queen, or
seen any **pirates** strolling down the street?
Have you checked out the
totally weird souvenirs
(like coconuts disguised as
snorkeling tropical fish)?

Wacky things are all over the place. See if you can find
a cupcake shop covered in **polka dots** and a great big tiki statue.

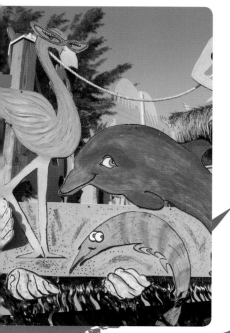

Jennifer Brinkman

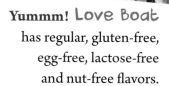

Yummm! Love Boat
has regular, gluten-free,
egg-free, lactose-free
and nut-free flavors.

45

Sand Castle Capital of the Universe

Each November, famous sand artists come from around the world to build **fantastical castles** on Fort Myers Beach. They also make **monkeys**, angels, **dinosaurs**, Roman chariots, fairy tale **princesses** and everything else you can imagine. When they're finished, there's a **fun festival** with music, food and even **castle-building lessons**.

It's never too soon to start practicing!

Picnic in the Park!

Estero Island, home of Fort Myers Beach, has **seven miles of beaches!** When you need a shady picnic spot, try a **chickee-shaded table** at **Newton Park**.

Lynn Hall Park and **Crescent Family Beach Park** are both next to the pier.

For barbecue grills, nature trails, game tables and more, the place to go is **Bowditch Point Park**.

Parasailing! It's the next best thing to having wings!

Smiley has the happiest face on the beach, don't you think? And no wonder! Parasailing is the next best thing to having your own wings to float in the air like a sea bird.

Any age can do it!

Paradise Parasail says if you can sit, you can fly. You start by sitting in a comfy swing chair on the boat, and before you know it, you're floating!

You'll want to stay up there forever, but landing is AWESOME too. Would you rather get a little bit wet (like maybe just dip your feet in the water), super-soaking wet (lots of fun!), or stay dry? If you're at least 90 pounds you can even fly solo.

← That means all by yourself!

The captains take lots of pictures and you can even have a close-up video of yourself in the air!

Parasails come in a **rainbow of colors**, all over Fort Myers Beach! You'll also see the colorful sails of Ranalli Parasail, Mid Island Watersports, Holiday Watersports, Estero Island Parasail and All Island Watersports.

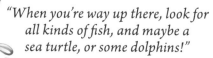

Paradise Parasail (2)

"When you're way up there, look for all kinds of fish, and maybe a sea turtle, or some dolphins!"

47

Meet the Dolphins aboard the Estero Bay Express

There are about **nine hundred and sixty two bajillion** fish, **birds,** tiny **shrimp, mollusks** and **crabs,** as well as **raccoons, manatees** and other **mammals** living in Estero Bay, its mangrove islands, super-shallow mud flats and sea grass beds. And best of all: **dolphins!**

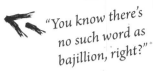

"You know there's no such word as bajillion, right?"

Hop aboard the catamaran Estero Bay Express II to watch for **Atlantic bottlenose dolphins jumping and playing in the bay.**

Can you believe it? The captains can recognize nearly all **80 dolphins in the pod** by their markings and the shapes of their dorsal fins. Maybe you'll meet our favorites, **Batman and Robin!** They know other **bizarro stuff,** too, like why a **pelican stands on her eggs.** (Because her webbed feet keeps them warm!)

Q: Why might a **seagull stand on a pelican's head?**

A: To steal fish right out of her beak!

QUIZ

What is a POD?
(a) A pile of peas
(b) A family of dolphins
(c) A music player

answer: b

48

Do you Wish to Fish?

Snook, redfish, sea trout, grouper, snapper—even sharks and barracuda—hang out in the estuaries of Estero Bay and in the Gulf of Mexico. Our friend Emma caught this pretty sea trout practically all by herself with a teeny bit of help from one of the salty old captains at Fish-Tale Marina.

Any way you want to fish, you have tons of choices. You can hop aboard a big boat for deep-sea fishing, fish right from the beach or the pier, or even go fishing with a guide in the middle of the night! Get a list of kid-friendly fishing guides from Roxie at Times Square.

Some restaurants will cook up your catch. But our favorite kind of fishing is catch-and-release!

Capt. Rob Modys

Mini Golf!

Is there any *ordinary* mini golf around here? No, Sir and No, Ma'am!

You can even feed baby alligators swimming around a pirate ship at Smuggler's Cove Adventure Golf.

And at Jungle Golf you'll feel like Tarzan and Jane, surrounded by elephants, rhinos, zebras and such. The grownups will be begging to play again and again!

ZOOM! FLY! Become A Real Sailor!

Teens and tweens ages 7 to 17 can take an awesome 5-day **Learn to Sail** course **free** with two paid adults at Steve and Doris Colgate's famous **Offshore Sailing School**. They also have fun **2-hour sailing lessons** for parents and kids.

This is at Pink Shell Beach Resort & Marina

Earn your official Conch Blower Certificate and get your picture in the **Conch Blower Hall of Fame** aboard the **FantaSea Sunset Celebration Cruise**.

Pass the test and get a diploma. Woo Hoo!

It's a dolphin! It's Aquaman! No, wait—it's YOU, Flyboard Kid!

Did you ever see a dolphin **burst** out of the water, **soar** into the air and then **dive** back down for an underwater swim? Maybe that's what flyboarding feels like. Except that you wear special boots, and instead of tail flukes, you're powered by a super-size water hose.

If you weigh at least 80 pounds, get the scoop at FMB Flyboard.

Families can rent sailboats, stand up paddleboards, Jet Skis, WaveRunners, pedal boats, kayaks and more cool stuff at beach stands all over the island. Some outfitters, like **Eco Paddlesportz**, deliver right to you.

How about a dolphin tour on WaveRunners? Check out **Holiday Adventure Tours!**

Meet a Pirate... or be one!

Actual pirates were fearsome bad guys, but the pirates of Fort Myers Beach are all about **outrageous fun.** You and your grownup mateys get **sworn in as pirates** to sail aboard the **Spanish galleon**, *Pieces of Eight,* along with its **scurvy crew: Poop Deck Pappy, Peg Leg Meg, Pick Pocket Pete** and the rest. There are games, **face painting**, pirate grog and grub, **secret treasure maps,** and plenty of **pirate booty.** Sign on at **Salty Sam's Marina.**

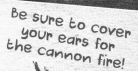

"Dare ye get yer picture taken with me?"

Be sure to cover your ears for the cannon fire!

"Avast, lads & lassies!
Ye dare not miss the **pirate ship battles** down at the seaport at **Ye Fort Myers Beach Pirate Fest.** It's me favorite weekend of the year. **Thar be a parade of dastardly pirates** and wenches, **costume contests, magic and puppet shows,** a **pie-eating** contest, **treasure hunts,** and plenty more shenanigans."

Whoa! Whose TRACKS are those? Whose NOSE is that? What makes those BIRDS PINK? Who LIVES there?

And other mysteries

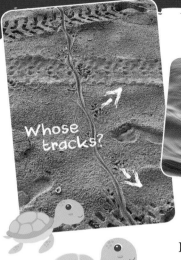

Whose tracks?

"besides me, of course"

Fort Myers Beach is part of a **splendiferous ecosystem** where **wondrous creatures** play, make nests, **burrow in the mud**, hunt and feed. To solve all these **mysteries** and more, sign up for an adventure with a **naturalist guide**. You can go dipnetting, shell collecting, kayaking and more at **Clearly Connected Nature Tours'** awesome three-hour kids camp. You get a special **Junior Naturalist certificate!**

Lee County VCB

Gaea Guides will take you paddling under a full moon! **Kayak Southwest Florida** has an awesome Sunday morning **family kayaking and shelling** trip at **Lovers Key.**

or...

How about a **catamaran ride** into the Gulf of Mexico, or to some **uninhabited islands** for shelling, **wildlife watching** and **dipnetting? Sight See-R Cruises** takes you **FREE on your birthday!**

Summer Camps!

Check out the cool day camp at **Ostego Bay Foundation Marine Science Center.** **Kayak Excursions** has a week-long **Kid Kayak Camp** at Bunche Beach Preserve.

Oooh, how about a Calusa Ghost Tour?

Not too scary!

You'll paddle to Mound Key, the center of the **ancient Calusa kingdom. Calusa John** tells **cool Calusa stories** and even brings along **weapons** and **masks.** or...

Wear your oldest muck-wading shoes and join a kayak tour into the **mysterious mangrove creeks** of Calusa lands. Sign up at **Mound House.**

John Paeno

What's THE GREAT CALUSA BLUEWAY?

It's a **super-long paddling trail** that winds in and out of rivers, creeks and along the beach. You can kayak, canoe, or SUP as long as you want, or **even camp for a whole week if you like!**

Grownup Tip: Calusa Blueway Trail guides, maps and the app are all free online.

Do you SUP?

Don't worry—it takes about **9 minutes and 4 seconds** to learn your balance on a **stand up paddleboard,** and then it's **sooooooooooooo easy and fun!**

don't forget your life jacket!

Michael Hammond/Lee County Parks & Recreation

What's the BEST THING about Lovers Key State Park?

Shutterstock

Sand-Sational Beach?

Eagles, Ospreys & Pelicans?

Burgers & Hot Dogs at Hurricane Charlie's?

Seagulls and Shorebirds?

Waverunner & Jet Ski Tours?

"Don't forget the roseate spoonbills

Bikes, Chairs & Umbrellas to Rent?

Free Ranger Activities?

Swimming & Snorkeling?

Picnic Spots?

Paddleboards to Rent?

Sailing & Supping?

Pretty Shells & Beach Treasures?

Fishing?

Fantabulous Kayaking & Canoeing?

Geocaching?

Alligator Pond?

SEA TURTLE CROSSING

Cool Bike Paths & Hiking Trails?

Marsh Bunnies, Ghost Crabs & Gopher Tortoises?

Junior Ranger Certificates?

Fun Tram Ride?

Manatees?

Dog Beach!
Near Lovers Key is a secret cove where pooches can play in the shallow water, dig holes in the sand and make new friends. And guess what? **No Leashes required** and it's free! Be sure to bring your doggies' beach toys and drinking water.

Beach Theater
Waiters serve you dinner (and dessert too) while you watch the movie!

Shutterstock

Beach Bowl & Pelican's Arcade
is a fun old-fashioned family place with food and games, too. Check out the crazy glow bowling, where the neon lighted pins rock and roll!

Two Good Ideas!
1. Take the bright blue and yellow trolley around the island. It's easy and kids under 12 are free

2. Rent a bike!
Fun 'N' Sun Rentals (*free delivery*)
Quicky Scooters & Bikes (*near Times Square*)

Land Ho! What's up on the Mainland?

"**Ahoy Mateys!** *Do ye love baseball? Head for the batting cages. Ye can watch Major League Baseball spring training, too, and cheer for me favorite home team.*

How'd ye like to peek inside Thomas Edison's secret laboratory? Or find out why that scallywag chewed on pianos and pulled all sorts of other shenanigans?

Feel like taking a go-kart ride or jumping around in a foam pit? Even an old sea dog like me might try out some ice skating. Arrrgh!

So, what are ye waiting for?

If yer in the mood to skip the beach for a day to ride a pony, feed a peacock, go to a festival or—shiver me timbers—cuddle a snake, turn the page and set sail for the mainland!"

Linwood Ferguson

Sunsplash Water Park

Birthday Party Alert!
Check out all the mainland attractions for **exciting** birthday **party ideas**.

Drop Anchor and Play, Play, Play!

Zoomers

You're barely off the islands and what do you see? The Cobra Coaster slithering around in the sky above Zoomers! This family amusement park has midway rides just for little kids, arcade games for bigger kids, go-karts and mini golf for every age, and more. You can get silly in the bumper boats and the Water Wars!

Lakes Regional Park

The problem with Lakes Regional Park is what to do first. It's a **dilemma!** There are **pedal boats, water toys, bikes, canoes and kayaks** to rent. Also, **two playgrounds, nature trails,** shady **picnic spots** (even grills!) and a **fishing lake.** You could spend the whole day! Be sure to pack a swimsuit to cool off on the splash pad! And guess what? Admission is FREE!

Train Village

All aboard the mini-train with a real engineer. You'll **chug through tunnels, over bridges,** into the woods and through a little village. Your ticket includes the Railroad Museum, too!

Castle Golf

Who loves **knights** and **castles** and enchanted forests? We do! Right next door to Lakes Regional Park is this **mystical, magical mini golf** park. Play day or knight. Tell the grownups and teenagers: no cheating on the score or it's the stocks for you!

Knight -get it?

The Greatest (and weirdest) Inventor Ever?

Three of Thomas Edison's favorite things to do were **figuring out inventions**, **listening to music** and **playing tricks** on people.

The inventions worked out well, as you know from his famous Light bulb. But he had more than 1,000 other inventions, too. He even figured out how to make **rubber tires** for the cars that his next door neighbor invented. **Who was his neighbor? Henry Ford!**

After testing 17,000 plants in his botanic laboratory, what was the secret ingredient to make rubber? A yellow weed called goldenrod!

Wait! Thomas Edison was mostly deaf, so how could he hear music? Easy! He could bite on the wood part of the piano or phonograph and "listen" to the vibrations! You can see the **bite marks** for yourself!

Laboratory

QUIZ
Thomas Edison invented
a. talking doll
b. x-ray machine
c. movie camera
d. microphone
e. record player
f. all the above

Answer: f

Visitors sometimes get to meet the "pretend" Thomas Edison!

Museum

So what kinds of tricks did he play on people?
Well, some say he once **fried some shoe leather for dinner** and said it was steak!

Check out **Thomas Edison's inventions** and some of **Henry Ford's cars** at the

Edison & Ford Winter Estates

The very first Ford car was a quadricycle!

EDISON FORD INVENTOR'S CAMP TODAY

You can have **mind-boggling**, **electrifying fun** on the **Young Inventors Tours**, and even go to **Inventor's Camp!** There's a restaurant and two gift shops, and also the most **huge-ariffic banyan tree** you've ever seen!

Did you know that Thomas Edison's **horse mowed the lawn?** Find out more **wacky stuff** when you visit the estates.

Check out the dates for the **petting zoo!**

Thomas Edison's House

Future Marine Biologist Alert!

Sign up ahead for a special **Marine Science Kids Cruise** aboard the **Edison Explorer.** Or take a regular **sightseeing cruise** on the Caloosahatchee River any time.

Pure Florida/ Merry Coffman

www.PureFortMyers.com

Butterflies love coreopsis, Florida's state wildflower (say it: Ko-Ree-**OP**-Sis).

Flutter on by!

If you're a frog or a **lizard**, don't even THINK about eating a monarch butterfly. It's poison to you. But if you're a kid, and a monarch butterfly lands on you, it's very **good luck!** Mostly they land on **flowers** to drink their delicious nectar.

The place to **meet native Florida butterflies**— like our state butterfly, the **Zebra Longwing**— is **The Butterfly Estates.** You can watch them fluttering around the flowers, see their **teeny, tiny eggs,** even watch them being born and **getting released** into nature!

Check out all the butterfly stuff (and **fudge too!**) in the shop.

The first Sunday of the month is **Sunday FUNday.** It's free, with activities and surprises for kids.

Zebra Longwing

Snowball

Cool Down!

It can get pretty steamy in a butterfly house, so afterward you can head to the **coldest spot in Fort Myers.** Five minutes away is the **Skatium** **ice skating** and **hockey rink.** They have **public skates** every day, and **skating lessons**, and special **family nights.** There's also a snack bar and a game arcade.

SWFL Museum of History

FORT MYERS FIRE DEPARTMENT

Ford Model T!

At the **Southwest Florida Museum of History,** you can see what a **fire truck** and **train car** looked like almost 100 years ago. The little museum also has exhibits about Paleo, Calusa and Seminole Indians, Conquistadors, **Civil War soldiers, pioneers** and **cowboys.**

"When fire trucks were pulled by horses, Dalmations helped keep the horses calm!"

Cowboys were called "**crackers**" because of the **sound their whips made** when they rounded up their cattle.

Imagine this!

What kind of **scientist** will you be? A **marine biologist**, a **meteorologist**, or perhaps a **physicist**?

What? You're just a kid and haven't decided yet?

That's okay! Just head over to the **Imaginarium Science Center** and test out some ideas! You can step right into the middle of a **hurricane** (a safe, dry one!). Forecast the weather on TV. Make **mysterious electrical currents** dance around when you touch the **plasma ball**.

LOOK!
Your own personal
lightning bolt!

Check out the special summer and holiday camps!

Have you ever seen a Madagascar **hissing cockroach?** Or watched a gecko clean its eyes with its tongue? Seriously, you can, at the **Imaginarium!** What else can you do? Try **science experiments,** watch a **3D dinosaur movie**, visit some **prairie dogs** and lots more.

Feed some stingrays (and touch them gently if you like).

City of Palms... and Art and Music

Thomas Edison loved **palm trees** so much that he gave the City of Fort Myers a **gazillion of them.** That's why it's called City of Palms.

Watch artists paint during Art Walk, the first Friday of each month. On the third Friday, it's **Music Walk,** with **singers** and **musicians.** It's free! And what else is free? Kids and teens activities and storytimes at the Fort Myers Regional Library!

Florida Repertory Theatre/Eric Coble

Do you Like plays? At the **Arcade Theatre,** you might sit in the very same spot where Thomas Edison watched the "talking movies" that he invented. At the **Broadway Palm Dinner Theatre** you get food with the play, and the Barbara B. Mann Performing Arts Center has big family shows.

Are You an Actor? Check out all the fun kids' camps and plays at the Alliance for the Arts, The Florida Repertory Theatre, and Sidney & Berne Davis Art Center's Theatre Kids.

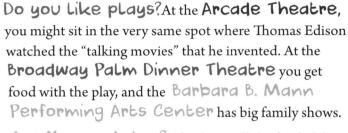

You can find out **more cool stuff** about soldiers, cowboys, and even hear some good old **ghost stories** on a True Tours walk around the River District. Or take a horse and carriage ride with Charlene's Classic Carriages.

Holiday House!

Mr. and Mrs. Edison went to holiday parties at their friends' houses, the Burroughs and Langford-Kingston Homes. They probably didn't **meet Santa,** but you can! And the **cookies are delicious!**

Picnic idea: Take your lunch to the playground at Centennial Park.

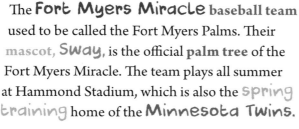

Linwood Ferguson

...and BASEBALL!

The **Fort Myers Miracle** baseball team used to be called the Fort Myers Palms. Their **mascot, Sway,** is the official **palm tree** of the Fort Myers Miracle. The team plays all summer at Hammond Stadium, which is also the spring training home of the **Minnesota Twins.**

Don't miss the bounce house and speed pitch in the Kids Zone!

Kids under 12: You can join the free Junior Miracle Kids Club and get free tickets, free popcorn, and even a birthday greeting from Sway!

Q. Who else has spring training in the City of Palms? Here's a clue!

A. Right! The **Boston Red Sox!** They play at Jet Blue Stadium. The mascot, Wally the Green Monster, has a **new little sister mascot,** Tessie, born in Fort Myers!

Stars and Asteroids and Meteors!
and snakes? and eyeballs?

At the Calusa Nature Center and Planetarium, you can visit **galaxies far, far away** through giant telescopes, and learn the **mysteries of the universe** under the 44-foot dome.

Freaky Factoid: Your **eye** is like a **small telescope** that can see about **5,000 stars** at a time! With a VERY LARGE telescope, maybe **48 bajillion.**

See the **live animal presentation** and visit rescued wild creatures in the Nature Center. There also are butterfly and bird aviaries and nature trails. **One admission covers both.**

Jump!

If you can walk you can jump, at **Sky Zone Trampoline Park**. It's soooo much fun, even for grownups. Little kids love Toddler Time. Big kids are crazy about Sky Slam basketball and Ultimate Dodgeball, and EVERYBODY loves the Foam Zone.

Attention Homeschoolers: Check out Sky Zone's Home School Hoppy Hour!

Bowl!

Anybody who thinks a bowling alley is just for bowling has absolutely, positively never been to a **Headpinz Entertainment Center!** It glows, sizzles and vibrates like an electric crayon box. There's laser tag, an aerial ropes course, giant arcade zones and our favorite, Glow Bowl.

PARTY!

What great places for birthday parties!

that's Tinkerbell

Ride!

Want to meet a **mini-horse, just 24 inches high?** That's how tall Stitch was when he was born at **Saddlewood Horse Club!** On **Horse Interaction Day**, you get to **ride, pet** and **groom** the ponies and horses, have lunch with them, and even **paint** them! It's once a month. Make reservations!

Skate!

Is rollerskating your favorite thing? Then Bamboozles is your place! They have skate lessons, arcade games, family skate times, homeschool skate parties and most important, the **Kids Skate Free Club!**

Hit a Homer!

Baseball or softball? Slow pitch or fast pitch? Whether you're a super slugger or just starting, you can practice in the batting cages at Mike Greenwell's Bat-A-Ball Family Fun Park. There's also an indoor arcade, go-karts, mini golf and carnival rides.

Shutterstock

Get a Hole-in-One!

Alico Family Golf has a cool program for all age kids (and grownups too) called SNAG. That stands for Starting New At Golf. Besides regular-size golf courses, they have driving ranges and lighted mini golf.

See Tons of Manatees!

And we do mean TONS!

Whoa! Look how many manatees you can see up close at one time at Manatee Park! It's their home in winter because of the warm water. Watch from the land or a kayak. The park also has a butterfly garden, fishing pier, playground, picnic areas, gift shop, kayak tours and kids activities.

Meet a Burrowing Owl!

The most adorable owls on the planet live in underground nests called burrows, all around Cape Coral. Get a map of their locations from Cape Coral Friends of Wildlife at the Rotary Park Environmental Center. Rotary Park also has a butterfly house, a nature trail, barbecue grills, a playground, and doggies can run off-leash at Wagging Tails Dog Park.

Q. What do burrowing owls eat?
   a. Cheetos, crackers, McDonalds fries.
   b. roaches, mice, frogs

A. You know the answer is b), right?
   Our junk food makes them sick.

Nancy Kilmartin

Karen DiNoto

65

A Shell Factory?
What's up with THAT?

What if you got a HUUUUGE empty box, and inside you put **peacocks**, some **bumper boats**, paddle boats, a **Tyrannosaurus Rex** and a bunch of his friends, a **pirate cove**, a **zip line**, **trampolines**, a gazillion decorated **Christmas trees**, a zoo with **400 live creatures** and a museum of **lions, grizzly bears, coyotes, rhinos and such**?

AND what if you **also** put inside the box a bunch of **arcade games**, a **merry-go round**, a **turtle pond** and 9,999,999,999,999 **seashells** from all over the world? Oh, and don't forget to put in restaurants, a **Sno-cone** stand, a fudge kitchen, a **Water Wars** game and a **mini golf course!**

AND what if you dumped the whole enormous box out around a lake? Well, you'd have **The Shell Factory**—the most **outrageous place** between here and **Mars. But that's not all!** Keep reading!

Soaring Eagle Zipline Inc.

"I hope he doesn't see me walking by!"

You can feed **Iggy Pop** the iguana, the peacocks, giant tortoises, weird birds and other creatures right out of your hand!

The Shell Factory has **doggie parties,** and **doggie church** on Sundays. And **Santa Claus** comes in **July!** The Shell Factory is also the **biggest gift shop** in the entire world. You'll have to check out this wacky place for yourself. Luckily, you don't have to go all the way to Mars!

Cute Sea Shell Owls

Huge wild animal museum

Chill Out!

Sunsplash Family Water Park is definitely the place to be on a hot summer day! **Little kids** will love the super-fun new **Pirate's Cove** and the family pool, while **fearless older kids** head straight for the big slides like **Thunder Bump**, **Terror Tube**, and **X-celerator**. Everybody loves **tube-floating** on the **Main Stream River**. Watch for special Family Fun Nights!

Paddle the Estero River!

Take a guided kayak trip with Florida Master Naturalists at **Koreshan National Historic Site**. This peaceful paddling trail is perfect for beginners. There's also a woodsy **campground**, hiking trails, picnic spots and an old settlement of **very strange pioneers**. They believed that the Earth is hollow and we live inside!

Mango Queen

Mango Throwing Champs

Go to a Festival!

From Thomas Edison's **giganto birthday party** (Edison Festival of Light) to a **mango-throwing contest** (MangoMania!), to a **medieval fair** with **sword fighting**, **jousting** and **magicians**, the fun never stops around these parts. **So check the calendar and get going!**

FESTIVALS! FAIRS! HAPPENINGS!

January
Medieval-Faire, Lakes Park **f**
Gumbo Fest, The Shell Factory **f**

February
Spring Training begins! **f**
Edison Festival of Light Parades & Events **f**
SWFL & Lee County Fair **f**
Burrowing Owl Festival **cc**

March
Calusa Heritage Day, Pine Island
Shrimp Festival & Parade **fmb**
St. Patrick's Day Parade **fmb**
Southwest Florida Reading Festival **f**
Spring Training all month! **f**

April
Easter Bunny Trail, Mike Greenwell's **cc**
Spring Festival, Children's Education Center **s**
Lighthouse Birthday Party, Boca Grande

May
Mother's Day: Freebies for Mom at several attractions!
Islands Night at Fort Myers Miracle **f**

June
National Seashell Day Shellabration **s, c, fmb**
Father's Day: Several attractions to take Dad free!
Battle on the Blueway SUP Race **fmb**
Gasparilla Island Kids Classic Tarpon Tournament

Sanibel = **s**
Captiva = **c**
Fort Myers = **f**
Cape Coral = **cc**
Fort Myers Beach = **fmb**

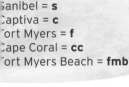

BATTLE ON
THE BLUEWAY
SUP RACE

Linwood Ferguson

Shutterstock

69

FESTIVALS! PARADES! FIREWORKS!

July
MangoMania Festival **cc**
Independence Day Parade & Fireworks **fmb, s**
4th of July Freedom Fest & Fireworks **f**
Ostego Bay Foundation 4th of July Fishing Tournament **fmb**

August
Community Day, Fish-Tale Marina **fmb**

Awesome family discounts ALL SUMMER!
**Check out all the cool summer camps, indoors & out!
Tons of awesome family discounts everywhere**

Jennifer Brinkm

October
Fort Myers Beach Pirate Fest
Zoomers Fall Festival **f**
Oktoberfest **cc**
"Ding" Darling Days **s**
Kiwanis KidsFest **cc**
Columbus Day Parade **cc**
Family Fright Night **fmb**
Haunted Hike, Mike Greenwell's **cc**
Haunted Walk & Friendly Forest, Calusa Nature Center **f**
Halloween along McGregor Blvd: luminaries, ghosts & treats **f**
Pumpkin Patch, Scarecrows & Halloween Express Train, Lakes Park **f**

HOLIDAYS! CELEBRATIONS!

Christine Rooney

November

American Sand Sculpting Championships **fmb**
"Ding" Darling Kids Fishing Derby, Sanibel Causeway
Cayo Costa Heritage Day
Coconut Festival, Sunsplash **cc**
Tree Lighting & Fireworks, Tween Waters **c**
Aviation Day, Page Field **f**

December

Great Outdoor Adventure Day, Lovers Key **fmb**
Sanibel Captiva Luminary Trail
Captiva Holiday Village & Golf Cart Parade
South Seas Holiday Stroll **c**
Captiva Cruises Lighted Boat Parade
Holiday Nights, Edison & Ford Estates **f**
Fort Myers Beach Boat Parade
Fireworks! **fmb, f, s**
Downtown Countdown & Junior Balloon Drop **f**
Holidays in the River District **f**
Holiday Express Train Ride, Lakes Park **f**

TELL THE GROWNUPS!

"Some years, an event can be either at the end of one month or the beginning of the next month. Always check the local listing."

Sanibel = **s**   Captiva = **c**   Fort Myers = **f**   Cape Coral = **cc**   Fort Myers Beach = **fmb**

TIME'S A-WASTIN', MATEYS! GET GOING!

A
Adventure Water Sports adventure-watersports.com (239) 849-6342
Adventures in Paradise adventureinparadiseinc.com (239) 472-8443
Alico Family Golf alicofamilygolf.com (239) 334-4653
All Island Watersports theislandwatersports.com (239) 765-1284
Alliance for the Arts (See Lee County Alliance for the Arts)
Arcade Theatre floridarep.org (239) 332-4488

B
Bailey-Matthews National Shell Museum shellmuseum.org (239) 395-2233
Bamboozles Skating & Event Center gobamboozles.com (239) 482-7789
Barbara B. Mann Performing Arts Hall bbmannpah.com (239) 481-4849
Beach Bowl FMB beachbowlandpelicansarcade.com (239) 466-3033
Beach Theater, Fort Myers Beach fmbtheater.com (239) 765-9000
BIG ARTS bigarts.org (239) 395-0900
Billy's Bikes and Rentals billysrentals.com/rentals (239) 472-5248
Boca Grande Lighthouse & Museum barrierislandparkssociety.org (941) 964-0060
Boston Red Sox floridagrapefruitleague.com/teams/redsox (877) 733-7699
Broadway Palm Children's Theater broadwaypalm.com (239) 278-4422
Bubble Room bubbleroomrestaurant.com (239) 472-5558
Burroughs Home & Gardens burroughshome.com (239) 337-0706
Burrowing Owls, Cape Coral Friends of Wildlife ccfriendsofwildlife.org (239) 980-2593
Butterfly Estates thebutterflyestates.com (239) 690-2359

C
Cabbage Key cabbagekey.com (239) 283-2278
Calusa Blueway Outfitters (See Manatee Park)
Calusa Ghost Tours & Kayak Rentals calusaghosttours.com (239) 221-8218
Calusa Nature Center & Planetarium calusanature.org (239) 275-3435
Captain Bubby's Island Tours captainbubbys.com (239) 245-7383
Captain Jack Boat Tours captainjackboattours.com (239) 222-9886
Captiva Cruises captivacruises.com (239) 472-5300
Castle Golf castle-golf.com (239) 489-1999
Cayo Costa Camping – reserveamerica.com (800) 326-3521
Clearly Connected Nature Tours clearlyconnectednaturetours.com (239) 672-5712
Coconut Festival cocofest.com
College of Life Foundation Hiking & Kayaking Tours collegeoflifefoundation.org (239) 992-2184
CROW- Clinic for the Rehabilitation of Wildlife crowclinic.org (239) 472-3644

D

"Ding" Darling National Wildlife Society dingdarlingsociety.org (239) 472-1100
Dog Beach leeparks.org (239) 707-1874

E

Eagle Cam (seasonal) swfleaglecam.com
Eco Paddlesportz ecopaddlesportz.com (239) 671-9326
Edison & Ford Winter Estates edisonfordwinterestates.org (239) 334-7419
Edison Explorer purefortmyers.com (239) 919-2965
Edison Festival of Light edisonfestival.org
Estero Bay Express Dolphin Tours esterobayexpress.com (239) 463-3600
Estero Island Parasail esteroislandparasail.com (239) 765-4386
Every Kid in a Park nps.gov/kids/index.cfm

F

FantaSea Sailing fantaseasailing.com (888) 582-9046
Finnimore's Bike & Beach Rentals finnimores.com (239) 472-5577
Fish-Tale Marina thefishtalemarina.com (239) 463-3600
Florida Inshore Xtream Charters floridainshorextream.com (941) 698-0323
Florida Repertory Theatre floridarep.org (239) 332-4488
Florida State Parks floridastateparks.org
FMB Flyboard fmbflyboard.com (239) 898-4063
Fort Myers Beach Pirate Festival fmbpiratefest.com
Fort Myers Beach Sand Sculpting fmbsandsculpting.com (239) 454-7500
Fort Myers Beach Shrimp Festival fortmyersbeachshrimpfestival.com
Fort Myers Beach Theater (See Beach Theater)
Fort Myers Miracle miraclebaseball.com (239) 768-4210
Fort Myers Princess fortmyersprincess.net (239) 765-8500
Fort Myers Regional Library leegov.com (239) 533-4600
Fort Myers River District myriverdistrict.com
Fun 'N' Sun Beach & Bike Rentals fortmyersbeachbikerentals.com (239) 728-7564
GAEA Guides gaeaguides.com (239) 694-5513

G

Gasparilla Island Kids Classic gasparillaislandkidsclassic.com (941) 964-0907
Gasparilla Outfitters (See Gasparilla Islands Kids Classic)
Good Time Charters goodtimecharter.com (239) 218-8014
Great Calusa Blueway calusablueway.com (239) 707-7981
Gulf Coast Kayak gulfcoastkayak.com (239) 283-1125

H

Hammond Stadium (See Fort Myers Miracle & Minnesota Twins)
HeadPinz Entertainment Center headpinz.com (239) 302-2155
Herb Strauss Theater box office bigarts.org (239) 472-6862
Holiday Water Sports holidaywatersportsfmb.com (239) 765-4386

I

I Love Shelling iloveshelling.com
Imaginarium Science Center i-sci.org (239) 321-7420
Island Bike 'N Beach islandbikenbeach.com (941) 964-0711
Island Cinema islandcinema.com (239) 472-1701
Island Girl Charters islandgirlcharters.com (239) 633-8142

J

Jensen's Marina gocaptiva.com (239) 472-5800
JetBlue Park (See Boston Red Sox)
Jungle Golf junglegolfminigolf.com (239) 466-9797

K

Kayak Excursions kayak-excursions.com (239) 297-7011
Kayak Southwest Florida kayakswfl.com (239) 963-7296
KidsSkateFree.com (See Bamboozles)
Koreshan Historic Site Kayak Tours (See College of Life Foundation)

L

Laboratory Theater laboratorytheaterflorida.com (239) 218-0481
Lady Chadwick (See Captiva Cruises)
Lakes Regional Park leeparks.org (239) 533-7575
Lee County Alliance for the Arts artinlee.org (239) 939-2787
Leoma Lovegrove Gallery leomalovegrove.com (239) 283-6453
Lovers Key Adventures & Events loverskeyadventures.com (239) 765-7788
Lovers Key State Park floridastateparks.org (239) 463-4588

M-N

Manatee Park - Calusa Blueway Outfitters leegov.com/parks (239) 481-4600
Mango Mania mangomaniafl.net
McCarthy's Marina mccarthysmarina.com (239) 472-5200
Mid-Island Watersports midislandwatersports.com (239) 765-0965
Mike Greenwell's Bat-A-Ball & Family Fun Park greenwellsfamilyfunpark.com (239) 574-4386
Minnesota Twins Spring Training floridagrapefruitleague.com/teams/twins (800) 338-9467
Miracle Baseball (See Fort Myers Miracle)
Mound House moundhouse.org (239) 765-0865

O

Offshore Sailing School, Fort Myers Beach offshoresailing.com (239) 454-1700
Ostego Bay Foundation Marine Science Center ostegobay.org (239) 765-8101

P

Paddle Board Sanibel paddleboardsanibel.com (239) 472-5577
Paradise Parasail paradiseparasail.com (239) 463-7272
Periwinkle Park & Campground sanibelcamping.com (239) 472-1433
Pieces of Eight Pirate Tours floridapiratecruise.com (239) 765-7272
Pirate Festival (See Fort Myers Beach Pirate Festival)
Pure Fort Myers purefortmyers.com (239) 919-2965

Q Quick! Go to Mostly Kids Guides Facebook page and like us!
Quicky Scooters & Bikes quickyscootersandbikes.com (239) 463-8000

 R Railroad Museum & Train Village rrmsf.org (239) 267-1905
Ranalli Parasail ranalliparasail.com (239) 565-5700
Randell Research Center flmnh.ufl.edu/rrc/ (239) 283-2062
Reel Intense Inshore Charters reelintenseinshore.com (941) 468-1618
Rotary Park Environmental Center capcoral.net (239) 549-4606

S Saddlewood Horse Club capehorses.com (239) 738-9300
Salty Sam's Marina & Waterfront Adventures saltysams.com (239) 463-7333
Sanibel Historical Museum & Village sanibelmuseum.org (239) 472-4648
Sanibel Sea School sanibelseaschool.org (239) 472-8585
Sanibel Thriller sanibelthriller.com (239) 472-2328
Sanibel-Captiva Conservation Foundation (See SCCF)
Santiva Salt Water Fishing sanibelcaptivafishing.com (239) 472-1779
Save the Manatee Club savethemanatee.org
SCCF Sanibel-Captiva Conservation Foundation sccf.org (239) 472-2329
Segway of Sanibel sanibelbike.com (239) 472-3620
Shell Factory and Nature Park shellfactory.com (239) 995-2141
Sidney & Berne Davis Art Center sbdac.com (239) 333-1933
SightSea-R Cruises sightseaflorida.com (239) 765-7272
Skatium fmskatium.org (239) 321-7509
Sky Zone Indoor Trampoline Park skyzone.com/fortmyers (239) 313-5448
Smugglers Cove Adventure Golf smugglersgolf.com (239) 466-5855
Southwest Florida Eagle Cam (See Eagle Cam)
Southwest Florida & Lee County Fair swflcfair.com (239) 543-8368
Sun Splash Family Waterpark sunsplashwaterpark.com (239) 574-0558

T Tarpon Bay Explorers Nature Tours tarponbayexplorers.com (239) 472-8900
Tropic Star Cruises tropicstaradventures.com (239) 283-0015
True Tours truetours.net (239) 945-0405
Tween Waters Inn & Marina tween-waters.com (239) 472-5161

 U-Z Wagging Tails Dog Park capecoral.net (239) 549-4606
Woof-a-Hatchee Dog Park leegov.com/parks (239) 432-2154
YOLO Watersports yolowatersports.com (239) 472-1296
Zoomers Amusement Park zoomersamusementpark.com (239) 481-9666

Visitor Information

Beaches

Causeway Beaches

Tiny islands along the Sanibel Causeway. Free parking!

Sanibel Island

Blind Pass Beach | 6497 Sanibel-Captiva Rd.

Bowman's Beach | 1700 Bowman's Beach Rd.

Lighthouse Beach & Pier | 112 Periwinkle Way

Gulfside Beach & City Park | 2001 Algiers Lane

Tarpon Beach | 111 Tarpon Bay Rd.

Captiva Island

Turner Beach at Blind Pass Bridge | 17200 Captiva Dr.

Andy Rosse Lane Beach | 11570 Andy Rosse Lane

Captiva Beach, extreme north end | 14790 Captiva Dr.

Fort Myers Beach

The Pier and Beach at Lynn Hall Park

Bowditch Point Regional Park | 50 Estero Blvd.
top of the island

Bunche Beach | 18201 John Morris Rd.
between Sanibel & Fort Myers Beach

Crescent Beach Family Park
1100 Estero Blvd.

Newton Park | 4650 Estero Blvd.

Plus! Beach access signs are
everywhere on the island!

Lovers Key State Park

8700 Estero Blvd.
just south of Fort Myers Beach

Practically Everything about Everything

Lee County Visitor & Convention Bureau
fortmyers-sanibel.com | (239) 338-3500

Southwest Florida International Airport

Welcome booths in all terminals!

Lee County Parks & Recreation

leeparks.org | (239) 533-7275

Sanibel & Captiva Islands

Sanibel-Captiva Chamber Visitor Center
1159 Causeway Rd. sanibel-captiva.org | (239) 472-1080

Gasparilla/Boca Grande, Cayo Costa, Lovers Key & Mound Key

Florida State Parks
floridastateparks.org | (941) 964-0375

Barrier Island Parks Society

barrierislandparkssociety.org | (941) 964-0060

Pine Island & Matlacha

Pine Island Chamber Visitor Center
pineislandchamber.org | (239) 283-0888
3640 SW Pine Island Road, Matlacha

Fort Myers Beach

Roxie: Fort Myers Beach Chamber on Wheels
at Times Square | (239) 233-3941

Greater Fort Myers Beach Chamber Visitor Center

1661 Estero Blvd. fortmyersbeach.org | (239) 454-7500

Fort Myers River District

myriverdistrict.com

STAR ATTRACTIONS

With appreciation and respect for the leaders of these outstanding attractions on Sanibel Island, Captiva Island, Fort Myers Beach and the mainland: Pam and Tom Cronin, Kathy and Al Durrett, Jodi and Neil Newton, Chris Pendleton, Lisa Wilson, The late Paul McCarthy, Lisa Sbuttoni, and the Stewart family: Evelyn, Craig, Josh, Noah and Audrey.

A special thank you to Tamara Pigott, Executive Director of the Lee County Visitor & Convention Bureau, for your invaluable wisdom, guidance, and support.

You have all raised the bar of excellence for family experiences in our region, providing a guiding light to those of us who serve the residents and visitors to these shores.

A bazillion thanks!

To the Warriors and Honorary Warriors of the Mostly Kids' Tribe

Benefactors

To Sandi Corace, the grownup who persuaded me to make this the next Mostly Kids' Guide, and then opened those very first doors.

To Art, Sandi and Dustyn Corace for generously providing the perfect island headquarters during our season of research. Your kindness is fathomless.

Wise Ones

To Lee Rose and Francesca Donlan at the Lee County VCB, and Barb Harrington representing the Sanibel-Captiva Chamber of Commerce, for your depth of knowledge and resources, and your lightning-fast responses to my emails and phone calls.

Art Peeps

To gifted illustrator Margie Olsen, creator of our newest spokescreatures, Freckles the hermit crab and Marigold the loggerhead turtle.

To Christine Rooney, Mind Reader

To Brad Sanders, Superhero

Sidekicks

To Kira Pirre, Best Intern Ever

To Randy Simmons, Mapmaker, Organizer, Offical Sno-cone Taster, and partner in adventure and misadventure. No two kids ever had more fun!

And Most Especially...

All the great kids who show up on these pages, and so many others we've met along the way. Thanks for being awesome!

About the Author

Vanessa Rogers

As a teenager, Karen T. Bartlett picked up her first angel wing on Sanibel Island and fell in love with the islands forever. She knew that she would one day live here on the Gulf of Mexico. She is an award-winning author of 12 destination **travel books** and hundreds of **travel articles and photos** in **magazines** and **newspapers** in several countries. She's a member of **ASMP,** the American Society of Media Photographers, and **SATW,** the Society of American Travel Writers.

Before becoming an author, she was president of an Atlanta, Georgia public relations agency. When her (now grownup) children were small, the family finally moved to Florida, and the adventures began! She writes from the point of view of a reporter, a storyteller, and especially a mom. **She loves to dance, go shelling, try yummy new foods and hang out with furry, fishy and feathery creatures.**

Love this book?

Find more splendiferous adventures and learn more outrageous stuff in "A (mostly) Kids' Guide to Naples, Marco Island & The Everglades."

What in the world are Swamp Buggy Races? Can you actually camp out with Seminole Indians? Is there really a Skunk Ape? Learn where to pet a baby alligator (Wooten's Everglades Airboat Tours), climb a humongous tree house (Naples Botanical Garden), do weird science (The Children's Museum of Naples), sail on a fancy yacht (Naples Princess), feed giraffes out of your hand (Naples Zoo), and tons more!

On sale at great bookstores and gift shops all over Southwest Florida.

79